BRITAIN IN OLD PHO7

HAMMERSMITH AND SHEPHERDS BUSH

The water chute at Playlands, White City, 1934. Playlands was situated on the eastern side of Wood Lane opposite White City Stadium. It offered many of the same pleasure ground attractions of the old White City exhibition site which had been close by (see pp. 142–3).

BRITAIN IN OLD PHOTOGRAPHS

HAMMERSMITH AND SHEPHERDS BUSH

JEROME FARRELL and
CHRISTINE BAYLISS

LONDON BOROUGH OF HAMMERSMITH AND FULHAM
ALAN SUTTON PUBLISHING LIMITED

Alan Sutton Publishing Limited
Phoenix Mill · Far Thrupp · Stroud
Gloucestershire · GL5 2BU

in association with the
London Borough of Hammersmith and
Fulham, Archives and Local History Centre

First published 1995

Cover photograph: tramway construction in
Goldhawk Road, 1898 (see p. 117)

British Library Cataloguing in Publication Data.
A catalogue record for this book is available from
the British Library.

ISBN 0-7509-0857-2

Typeset in 9/10 Sabon.
Typesetting and origination by
Alan Sutton Publishing Limited.
Printed in Great Britain by
Ebenezer Baylis, Worcester.

Lower Mall from Hammersmith Bridge, 1907.

Contents

Members of the Women's Rowing Section of the Lyons' Club preparing before a training session for the Head of the River Race, 1936. The rowers were employees of J. Lyons & Co., who had their manufacturing premises at Cadby Hall, Hammersmith Road – near Olympia – from 1894. After a number of years of uncertainty Cadby Hall was demolished; homes and offices were built on the site.

Introduction

Only a mile separates Hammersmith Broadway from Shepherds Bush Green, and although the two areas have maintained their separate identities, they have always been closely linked. For centuries they formed the northern half of the manor and parish of Fulham, but from the time of Charles I onwards they had in practice a considerable degree of administrative independence from Fulham. This situation was eventually formalized by the establishment of Hammersmith as a separate civil parish in 1834. Throughout the period covered by this book, Hammersmith and Shepherds Bush formed a single unit of local government, controlled first by Hammersmith Vestry and then from 1900 by the Metropolitan Borough of Hammersmith. It was only in 1965 that the boundaries of the original manor and parish of Fulham were reconstituted with the creation of the London Borough of Hammersmith (later the London Borough of Hammersmith and Fulham).

The history and development of this area have inevitably been greatly influenced by its proximity to the ancient cities of London and Westminster. Important arterial roads from the west lead to these major centres of population through Hammersmith and Shepherds Bush, and over the years untold numbers of no doubt weary travellers have passed through here on the Great West Road, Goldhawk Road, Uxbridge Road and Westway, or crossed the Thames via Hammersmith Bridge.

The river itself has long been an important factor in Hammersmith life, as can be seen in the photographs in section 1. Used for fishing in earlier times, commercial and leisure activities predominated during the period this book covers; although today far less river traffic passes by, pleasure boats, rowers and of course the famous University Boat Race can still be seen from the Hammersmith riverside.

Improvements in public transport, depicted in section 7, together with the vast increase in the population of the metropolis, led to most of Hammersmith and Shepherds Bush becoming built up in the Victorian era, though north of Uxbridge Road development mostly took place somewhat later. The population figures speak for themselves – 24,000 residents of Hammersmith and Shepherds Bush in 1861, but over 135,000 people living in the same area by 1931 (by 1991 this figure had almost halved, to around 72,000). A comparison of the Ordnance Survey maps of the 1860s and 1890s shows the phenomenal amount of building carried out in that period in particular, when most of the pattern of streets still with us was established. Much of the open land around Hammersmith and Shepherds Bush, which was used largely for market gardens that supplied fresh produce to the London markets, and for plant nurseries and for brick fields, was consequently swallowed up in the immense conurbation of London. The majority of the photographs in this book, therefore, reflect a densely populated urban existence and an area of considerable commercial and industrial activity, though sections 5 and 6 include a few vestiges of disappearing rural ways, with scenes of sheep, haymaking and a thatched cottage.

Over the past 100 years both Hammersmith and Shepherds Bush have played a significant role as favourite places for Londoners to go to for entertainment, sport and leisure, as section 11 shows. Although the White City exhibitions and sports facilities depicted here have gone, and most of the cinemas have closed, people are still drawn to the area by its venues for live music and dancing, theatres, events at Olympia, the Linford Christie Stadium and the football at QPR.

The first half of this book has been arranged by area, working northwards from the riverside through to College Park. Since many of the photographs deal with certain specific issues, however – transport, education, work, war, entertainment and special occasions – the second half has been arranged on a thematic basis. Some of the views, such as those of Upper and Lower Mall and Hammersmith Bridge, are remarkably unchanged today; others have totally vanished, like those of Hammersmith Creek (now underneath Furnivall Gardens) and of many of the old buildings in King Street, Hammersmith Road and around Shepherds Bush Green, since replaced by modern shops and offices.

A number of the photographs record good times – boating on the lake in Ravenscourt Park, enjoying the attractions of White City and Playlands, various sporting and leisure pursuits, and festive occasions. Others – people sleeping rough on Shepherds Bush Green, poor housing conditions, Wormwood Scrubs prison and the destruction wrought by the bombs of the Second World War – remind us to be wary of having too rosy an image of the past.

Change and continuity. Both themes run through this book, and are omnipresent in today's Hammersmith and Shepherds Bush. Nowhere epitomizes this better than the Hammersmith Broadway vicinity itself, with its juxtaposition of old and new. Here are the constantly busy Hammersmith flyover, the 1990s Broadway Centre development, the state-of-the-art Ark building and the new West London magistrates court; yet here too stands St Paul's Church – the Victorian successor to the original seventeenth-century chapel, which had formed the spiritual and social focal point for Hammersmith for over 200 years and which is shown in a rare photograph in section 2. Also nearby, in the middle of the Broadway traffic, is Bradmore House, its fine early eighteenth-century façade recently restored after a chequered history (see p. 35). Continuity and change, everywhere.

Every picture tells a story, and a photograph conveys an immediate and direct impression of the past in a way rarely achieved by the written record. This book cannot tell the full, fascinating story of Hammersmith and Shepherds Bush, however. Their histories stretch back over many centuries, while photographic records only date from the mid-nineteenth century, a period of perhaps four or five generations. All the photographs here have been selected from the collection of over 60,000 held at Hammersmith and Fulham's Archives and Local History Centre, which also houses over two miles of original records relating to this locality from the fifteenth century onwards, as well as quantities of printed books, pamphlets and maps – a treasure house of local history for those who wish to delve deeper into the past. We hope this book will interest those who live, work or know this lively part of West London, and might also encourage some to explore its rich and varied past further.

Section One

FROM THE RIVER
TO KING STREET

Upper Mall, 1896. Kelmscott House is the large property in the foreground. William Morris (1834–96), the immensely gifted poet, designer, manufacturer and socialist, lived here from 1878 until his death (see also p. 154). While here he founded the Kelmscott Press, for which he designed founts of type, ornamental letters and borders.

The Furnivall Sculling Club, formerly Hammersmith Girls' Sculling Club, being coxed and coached by their founder, Dr F.J. Furnivall, 1907. The club was founded in 1896. Dr Furnivall was also founder of the National Amateur Rowing Association (later the Amateur Rowing Association).

Hammersmith Oil Mills and Upper Mall from the river, 1904. Houses and open spaces now occupy most of the industrial sites.

Lower Mall, possibly on a regatta day, early this century. Kent House, the headquarters of the Amateur Rowing Association, founded in 1891, is on the right. The tall chimney of Clark's Phoenix Lead Mills can be seen in the background of the photograph. The Lead Mills were destroyed by bombs in July 1944.

Upper Mall looking west from Rivercourt Road, *c.* 1900. Rivercourt House, which was then occupied by St Catherine's College, was purchased in 1951 for use as a prep school for Latymer Upper School. The elm trees were reputedly planted during the time of Queen Catherine of Braganza (1638–1705), consort of Charles II, who had lived nearby.

The Stork training ship, moored opposite 46–8 Upper Mall, was home to trainee naval cadets from 1913 until the ship was scrapped in 1950. In 1913 it was described as 'a training ship for convict boys out of the slums'.

At 1 a.m. on 7 January 1928 the Thames topped the river wall and flooded much of Hammersmith's riverside area. Sections of the wall were swept away, as at Lower Mall (above), and two servant girls were drowned in their basement bedroom in Upper Mall.

Thames barges being unloaded to the south of Hammersmith Bridge. This photograph gives some idea of the amount of commercial activity on the Thames at Hammersmith in the early 1900s. From this position on the bridge today you would see the offices of Compass Healthcare Ltd (occupied until recently by Rosser & Russell Building Services) and the Riverside Studios, the arts centre.

The Old Ship, 25 Upper Mall, mid-1890s. The remains of the porch of the original pub, believed to be seventeenth-century, can be seen below the pub sign in the background.

Children playing in Lower Mall, to the south of Hammersmith Bridge, probably in the Edwardian period. A garden now occupies the site of the small houses that used to stand along this stretch of the riverside.

The Oxford and Cambridge Universities Boat Race, 30 March 1895, from the Barnes towpath: Oxford won. This famous annual race, instituted in 1829, usually takes place in the latter part of March or the beginning of April, and covers a distance of a little over four miles on the Thames, from Putney Bridge to Mortlake.

An unusual photograph of the Boat Race, *c.* 1908–14. Spectators are being brought ashore from the barges from which they had watched the race.

Crowds occupying every spare inch of space along the riverside between Digby
Mansions and Hammersmith Bridge in an attempt to see the 1914 Boat Race, which
was won by Cambridge.

'One of the last of the Thames Steamboats to ply regularly on the Thames – the Thames at very low tide.' The writer of the note on the back of this photograph, believed to be William Bull (MP for Hammersmith, later Hammersmith South, 1900–28), adds 'people will scarcely believe I once forded the Thames (on tip toe it is true)'. As the last regular steamboat ran in 1905 this photograph probably dates from around 1903–5.

Taking the dog for a ride. Pony and trap with lady driver and a small dog in Rivercourt Road, which is now divided by the Great West Road. The Great West Road, built in the 1950s and early 1960s, cut through many roads and also the grounds of Latymer Upper School and Kelmscott House.

Regatta Day on Lower Mall, 1913. Special seating was constructed for spectators on the roof of the West End Amateur Rowing Association's premises. The public house on the right of the photograph is The Rutland, which had its own wharf and boat, plus seating for spectators on the roof – although it does not seem to have been used on this occasion.

The approach to Hammersmith Bridge with Digby Mansions on the right, 1910. An early motor car can be seen in the picture, along with a gentleman in a bath chair by the fountain. The cobbled road which he has just traversed must have given him an uncomfortable ride.

Palmer's Stores, the Hammersmith Bridge Road frontage, *c.* 1910. Originally founded in 1886 by Mr A.J. Palmer as a butchers and provisions shop, this store expanded over the years to become a well-known department store. It closed on 20 June 1953, after the business was purchased by Littlewoods.

Crossing Hammersmith Bridge in 1908. The bridge was designed by Sir Joseph Bazalgette and opened in 1887, using the piers of an older suspension bridge that had been built some sixty years earlier.

Hammersmith Creek, with Sankey's Yard on the right and a heavily loaded barge in the distance, probably in the late Victorian period.

Culverting the creek prior to the building of Hammersmith Town Hall, 1936. The Regal Cinema (now MGM Cinema), which opened in September 1936, can be seen in the course of construction.

A busy day on the creek with barges unloading, *c.* 1919–24. Barges could take their loads from the river up to King Street for local transportation. The site now forms part of Furnivall Gardens which opened on 5 May 1951.

The High Bridge over Hammersmith Creek, looking west from Henrietta Place into Doves Place, probably early this century.

Amy Adamson and her son John outside the family shop at 42 Marryat Street, *c.* 1913. Marryat Street has since disappeared; the site is now occupied by flats (Aspen Gardens) and part of the Great West Road.

Trafalgar Street, a small turning off Henrietta Place, *c.* 1900. Living conditions in terraces of small houses like these must have been very cramped by modern standards; the 1891 census records 213 people living in the 22 houses in this street. Much of the area near Trafalgar Street was demolished after the First World War and the Riverside Gardens flats were built on the site. The Great West Road now covers the site of this small street.

St Peter's Church and The Black Lion in Black Lion Lane, in the early 1880s. St Peter's, which was built 1827–9, is the oldest surviving church in the borough.

St Peter's Square, *c*. 1920. The square was saved from developers by the Borough Council and it was formally opened to the public on 29 April 1915 (see p. 151). The bronze figure of a Greek athlete which now stands in the open space was a gift from the family of the sculptor, Sir William B. Richmond, in 1926.

An 1896 view from Queen Street (now Queen Caroline Street) into Bridge Road. Queen Street, which runs into Hammersmith Broadway, took its name from Queen Caroline, consort of George IV, who had lived for a short while at Brandenburgh House. The royal marriage was an unhappy one; after years of living apart from her husband on the continent she returned to England when he succeeded to the throne, but was locked out of Westminster Abbey during the coronation of her estranged husband. She died shortly afterwards in Hammersmith. George Francis and Richard Honey, the two men who were killed during the disturbance following her death, in 1821, were buried in St Paul's Churchyard near by.

Queen Street, looking towards Hammersmith Broadway, after 1908. The police station, in the centre of the picture, was built in the 1860s. It was replaced by a more modern police station, completed in 1940, in Brook Green Road (now Shepherds Bush Road).

KING STREET AND THE BROADWAY

Hammersmith Broadway in the late Victorian period, looking towards King Street. The pub and other properties to the right of the photograph were demolished when the Broadway was widened in 1911.

Two-way traffic in King Street, *c.* 1904. The one-way system involving King Street, Glenthorne Road and Beadon Road was instituted during the Second World War, after bomb damage. The system was so successful that it remains in operation.

King Street has long been Hammersmith's main shopping street. This shows part of the road near the junction with Dalling Road, *c.* 1913. The eastern corner of this turning is still known as Selden's Corner.

The Hop-Poles Hotel in King Street. The decorations on the pub were to mark the route of Edward VII, who drove down King Street on his way to open the new Kew Bridge on 20 May 1903. They were arranged by John East, the manager of the nearby Lyric Theatre.

The spire of Rivercourt Methodist Church, built in 1875 to the design of Charles Bell, is still a landmark in this part of King Street. This photograph is thought to date from about 1910.

Charabanc party about to leave The Windsor Castle in King Street on 21 July 1898, with a trumpeter to see them off. The pub, which was located between Argyle Place and Galena Road, is known to have been in existence since at least 1753. Just before the Second World War the pub was rebuilt, its frontage being extended several feet forwards. In the early 1960s Tesco converted the property into a supermarket.

Another view of The Windsor Castle, *c.* 1895. The building to the left was occupied for a time by the London General Omnibus Company Ltd.

The Hampshire Hog, another of the many pubs in King Street, in 1880, with Hog Lane and part of the grounds of Rivercourt House to its right.

West End Baptist Church, King Street. The posters outside the church advertise meetings of the PSA – the Pleasant Sunday Afternoon Brotherhood. This was launched in 1893 by the pastor, Revd W. Page, who preached his last sermon on 26 January 1896 after a ministry of twenty years. In 1972 a more modern church opened and the old building was subsequently demolished; the Polish Cultural Centre now stands on the site.

Young's Corner at the junction of King Street and Goldhawk Road, probably in the early 1890s. The name derives from a grocer's shop (later an art dealer's shop) that used to stand on the corner. This building was demolished in 1893.

The bus station, in the centre of this view of Queen Caroline Street, was formerly part of Bradmore House, a private house built about 1710 which was later used as a school. Most of Bradmore House was demolished in 1913 but this elegant garden front was saved and re-sited as part of the London General Omnibus Company's bus station. In the redevelopment of Hammersmith Broadway in the early 1990s the front was again saved to become part of the reconstructed Bradmore House, now a restaurant. This photograph was probably taken during, or shortly after, the First World War.

A rare photograph of the original St Paul's Church, erected in 1629–31 as a chapel-of-ease to All Saints, Fulham. Its replacement, which looms over the Hammersmith flyover, was consecrated in 1883. The photograph is thought to date from about 1870.

Vine Cottage with St Paul's Church in the background, *c.* 1896. The cottage took its name from the vines there which were believed, in 1936, to have been planted some 300 years earlier. About 200 bunches of grapes were harvested in 1936. The cottage was demolished shortly before the Second World War and part of the Hammersmith flyover now crosses the site.

Hammersmith Broadway just prior to the demolition and rebuilding of The Swan, which was completed in late 1902.

An aerial view of Hammersmith Broadway and its surroundings, *c.* 1930. St Paul's Church can be clearly seen; the Broadway is in the centre of the photograph. It shows the road layout before the changes of the late 1950s – when Butterwick was created to link Hammersmith Road and Great Church Lane, thus completing the one-way system around the Broadway – and those of the 1960s, when the Hammersmith flyover was built to alleviate traffic congestion in the area.

Parked vehicles in the Broadway in 1908. The first Hammersmith Town Hall, opened in 1897 by the Duke and Duchess of Fife, cost £25,000 and was built by George Wimpey & Co. It stood near the junction of Brook Green Road (now Shepherds Bush Road) and the Broadway, and was demolished in 1962.

Another view of the Broadway, taken during its widening in 1911. Two pubs and a cinema were among the buildings demolished. The new George can be seen being built behind its predecessor. This view was taken sixteen days before the old George finally closed on 18 August 1911.

Hammersmith Broadway looking east towards Hammersmith Road, *c.* 1905. Part of the convent and school of the Sacred Heart can be seen in the distance.

The imposing Royal Sussex Arms in Hammersmith Broadway took its name from the Duke of Sussex, who laid the foundation stone of the first Hammersmith Bridge on 7 May 1825. Celebrations were held afterwards at the Hammersmith Coffee House, which was later renamed in the Duke's honour. The Broadway Electric Theatre, offering 'animated singing pictures', can be seen on the right of the photograph; it had a short life of about three years before it was demolished in 1911, so the photograph must date from around 1908–11.

FROM KING STREET TO GOLDHAWK ROAD

Goldhawk Road, looking west, in the 1920s. This photograph was taken close to the junction with Hammersmith Grove. The fish shop on the right not only sells fish and chips but is also offering 'live fish' for sale.

Ravenscourt Park House, a Georgian house built on the site of a much earlier property. The house was to become Hammersmith's first public library, formally opened in March 1890. The librarian, Samuel Martin, was paid the substantial salary of £130 per annum.

Ravenscourt Park on a summer's day, probably towards the end of the Victorian era. The park – covering 32 acres – and the mansion were acquired by the Metropolitan Board of Works (later London County Council) and Hammersmith Vestry in 1887 for £58,000. It was informally opened to the public on 19 May 1888.

Boating on the lake at Ravenscourt Park in 1930. The library, which can be seen in the background, was badly damaged by bombs in January 1941 and had to be demolished. After the war the conservatory survived as a shelter from the rain but was eventually pulled down.

The lake and bandstand at Ravenscourt Park in the grip of winter, probably in the late Victorian or Edwardian years. The lake, which had been empty when the estate was acquired, became a very popular attraction when it was filled and rowing boats were provided. Concerts were regularly held at the bandstand on Thursday and Sunday in the summer months.

Mr Venables, the Ravenscourt Park superintendent (back row, third from left and wearing a bowler hat) with his staff in September 1930.

Flooding under the railway bridge in Trussley Road (between Hammersmith Grove and Sulgrave Road), *c*. 1925. The embanked footpath on the right-hand side of the road would seem to indicate that flooding here was a regular occurrence.

The police section house at the junction of Dalling Road and Paddenswick Road, *c.* 1915–17. Batey & Co. Ltd, whose advertisement can be seen in the picture, had their mineral water works in Munster Road, Fulham.

Nos 10–16 Grove Mews, *c.* 1906–11. Finch & Sons, oil merchants, occupied nos 10 and 11 for several years and expanded into no. 9 from 1912.

Glenthorne Road at its junction with Cambridge Grove, showing St John's Church on the left, *c.* 1909. The driver of the no. 133 tram is busy adjusting the rear indicator blind ready for the journey to Kew Bridge.

Cambridge Road (now Cambridge Grove) during the Edwardian period. A District Line train is crossing the railway bridge in the centre of the picture.

Glenthorne Road looking east towards St John's Church. In 1901 the London County Council started the electrification of its tram services using conduit track instead of the overhead trolley distribution service; this photograph was probably taken soon after that date.

Clergy and choir of an unidentified local church, thought to be St John's in Glenthorne Road, *c.* 1928–31.

An electric tramcar on Beadon Hill, autumn 1930. The off-licence on the right of the picture is advertising a production of *Jew Suss* at the King's Theatre in Hammersmith, starring Matheson Lang, commencing 22 September 1930.

Flower sellers under the railway bridge in Goldhawk Road, *c.* 1907.

Goldhawk Road in 1902. The photographer's mother, Mrs Shiers, is shown on the right of this picture.

AROUND BROOK GREEN

The council's horse-drawn mowing machine at work on Brook Green in May 1939. This horse was probably one of the last employed by the council, which had only eleven horses left by 1935.

The West London Hospital in Hammersmith Road, *c.* 1905. Founded in 1856 in a six-roomed house nearby, this site was purchased in 1860. The hospital was extended several times but closed early in 1993.

Some of the elderly persons cared for by the Poor Sisters of Nazareth at Nazareth House, photographed around the turn of the century. This congregation of nuns commenced officially in 1864, although its origins go back to 1851 when five sisters left Paris and came to England. Their work continues in Hammersmith today.

The Vestry Hall, predecessor of Hammersmith Town Hall, in Brook Green Road (now Shepherds Bush Road), c. 1888–96. The building, formerly an old family house used for a number of years as a private school, was rented by the Fulham Board of Works as offices from 1856 until 1878, when it was practically reconstructed. The site was redeveloped less than twenty years later, the first Hammersmith Town Hall being opened on this site in 1897.

Brook Green Road (now Shepherds Bush Road) with the Broadway Congregational Church and fire station on the left and Hammersmith Central Library and the town hall on the right. In the centre of this photograph, which was taken around 1905–8 from near the junction with Hammersmith Broadway, a horse-drawn fire engine returning from a call-out can just be seen.

The Red Cow in Hammersmith Road, 1892. Its somewhat quaint, informal appearance was admired less in the late Victorian period than it might be today. In June 1898, when its replacement was completed, a local newspaper reported that 'The old "Red Cow" will no longer be an eyesore to the fastidious . . .'.

The Brook Green Laundry at nos 4 and 5 Brook Green was owned by the Graham Brothers. This photograph was taken in the 1920s. The business moved to Ravenscourt Park around 1928.

Slater's Buildings, Brook Green Place, 1910. Within a few years of this photograph having been taken the site was built over by extensions to Cadby Hall, a former piano factory, as part of the headquarters of J. Lyons & Co., the food and drinks manufacturers.

Hanover Cottages, probably in 1937, shortly before their demolition. The cottages were reached from a narrow passageway off Hammersmith Road, almost opposite the West London Hospital. A clearance order for the demolition of these cottages was issued in June 1936; the council allowed themselves seventeen months to rehouse the occupants.

Lakeside Road before renovations were carried out in the early 1950s. The kitchen range would have provided heat for this room, although its cooking facilities would have been superseded by the gas cooker in the corner. A small tin bath is wedged between the wall and cooker. Lakeside Road was originally named Wharton Road. In 1907 it was renamed Rayleigh Road and forty years later became Lakeside Road. The name derives from one of the lakes formed by the removal of brick earth; there were a number of such lakes in Hammersmith before they were filled in.

No. 112 Hammersmith Road, taken on 3 October 1931. Samuel Martin, the borough librarian, can be seen standing outside the house that had once been the home of Charles Keene, the artist.

STARCH GREEN TO

SHEPHERDS BUSH

Sheep in Shepherds Bush Road, 1905, crossing the line of the London and South Western Railway. The long, low, white building in the background was the last of the temporary buildings housing the Shepherds Bush Baptist Tabernacle. The present church was opened in 1907.

The pond at Starch Green, *c.* 1900. This small open space with a pond was situated at the junction of Goldhawk Road and Askew Road. A programme of gradual in-filling began in 1924, and a seat was placed on the extra open space created in 1929.

The back of houses in Becklow Road, *c.* 1946–7, shortly before their demolition. The Anderson shelters in the garden are a relic of the Second World War and were probably used, for a time, as garden sheds.

The junction of Paddenswick Road, Goldhawk Road and Greenside Road looking towards Starch Green, *c.* 1911. This junction was known as Seven Stars Corner from the nearby public house. The edge of the pub sign is visible on the left.

The entertainment centre of Shepherds Bush, *c.* 1924. The Shepherds Bush Empire on the left, which opened in 1903 and could seat 2,332 people, was designed by Frank Matcham. In the centre of the photograph is the Palladium Cinema, with the rather smaller capacity of 763. It had several names from its opening in *c.* 1910 – Cinematographic Theatre, Essoldo Cinema and in later years Odeon 2 and Classic Cinema. The Shepherds Bush Pavilion, on the far right, was designed by Frank Verity and opened on 16 August 1923 with seating for over 3,000 people. It was badly damaged by bombs on 8 July 1944 and had to be reconstructed, opening as the new Gaumont Cinema on 25 July 1955, when John Mills and Alistair Sim were among several screen stars who attended the gala event.

Nos 65–75 Shepherds Bush Green, formerly known as The Lawn, immediately to the north of the Shepherds Bush Pavilion. These houses have all disappeared and Shepherds Bush post office now occupies part of this site. The photograph dates from the 1920s or 1930s.

Syndercombe's Cottage on a snowy day prior to its demolition in 1891. Miles Syndercombe allegedly planned to ambush and assassinate Oliver Cromwell as he passed by here in January 1657. The plot miscarried, but Syndercombe died in the Tower of London in mysterious circumstances, possibly committing suicide, before the date of his execution. His corpse, however, was still hanged, drawn and quartered. The Bush Hotel and Theatre now stands on this site.

64 Shepherds Bush Green, previously part of The Lawn or Lawn Place, photographed before 1923. It was said to have been the residence of John Moody (1727?–1812), the actor, who lived here after his retirement from the stage in 1796. The site of the house is now occupied by the Shepherds Bush Odeon, formerly The Gaumont.

Rockley Road, prior to 1918. St Simon's Church was designed by the Victorian architect Arthur William Blomfield. The first part of the church was consecrated in 1880, the spire was completed in 1886 and the whole building was finally dedicated in 1897.

The Wellington Arms, situated on the north side of Shepherds Bush Green, *c.* 1900. The old inn, which was rebuilt in 1905, had a tea garden in its grounds. The *West London Advertiser* described it in 1905 as being 'a refuge for thirsty cricketers who ran in for refreshment from the ancient common land opposite'.

The Gaumont Studios in Lime Grove, *c.* 1915. The studios opened in 1913 and were used for filming; they closed thirteen years later for enlargement and improvement. From 1928 they were the home of Gainsborough Pictures. The BBC purchased the building in 1949 and used it until recently for the production of television programmes. New flats now stand on the site.

Sleeping out on Shepherds Bush Green, 1910. This area was described as 'a plague spot of London'. In 1907 a Salvation Army officer reported that on one occasion he had counted 170 men, women and children there. Proposals followed to enclose the green so that it could be 'closed' at night; but several years later the problem of it being 'by day and night a resting place for undesirable persons of both sexes' was unresolved. Thirty-two men and women were arrested there in one week in 1912. In many cases they were sentenced to three days hard labour.

UXBRIDGE ROAD
TO COLLEGE PARK

*Old cottages near the Shepherds Bush end of Wood Lane, c. 1889. A drawing very similar
to this photograph of a 'not very ambitious row of dwellings' was published in Kemp's
West London Sketcher and Theleme of 16 July 1889. Note the inclusion in this
photograph of a bicycle, which would have been a prized possession at this date.*

Shops in Uxbridge Road at the junction with Wood Lane, 1885–94. The sign on the white building in Wood Lane warns passers-by to 'Beware of the steamroller in the thoroughfare'.

The Queen Adelaide in Uxbridge Road close to Oaklands Congregational Church, possibly photographed in the latter part of the last century. The Denington family were licensees here for well over thirty years. The greenhouses beyond the pub probably belonged to one of the nurseries in Willow Vale.

Uxbridge Road, *c.* 1902–3. A pointing hand in the centre of the railway bridge indicates the location of Shepherds Bush Metropolitan Line station. This was in the middle of what is now Shepherds Bush Market. When the market opened in 1914 in the access road to the station, the station was closed and two replacement stations, Goldhawk Road and Shepherds Bush, were opened at either end of the market.

Protest in favour of a 30 m.p.h. speed limit on Westway, January 1937. Then, as now, speeding motorists caused problems in an area with a high proportion of children. This protest followed an accident to Patricia Geard, aged six, who died crossing the road on her way home from Sunday School on 27 December 1936, and a number of earlier accidents.

A thatched cottage near Wood House, Wood Lane. Wood House was a large property on the east side of Wood Lane, the site of which is now occupied by London Underground. The style of the clothes in this photograph suggests a date in the late Victorian period, when parts of Shepherds Bush still retained a semi-rural feel.

Construction of the Wormholt Estate, c. 1920. The original scheme was for houses to be offered to local ex-servicemen, with one third being made available for sale to local residents. By January 1923, 551 houses had been completed and were occupied. The scheme to sell houses was not too successful, as only fifty-three had by then been disposed of to purchaser-tenants.

Wormwood Scrubs prison, *c.* 1902. It was built by prisoners. Work started in 1874 and was completed in 1891. Thirty-five million bricks were made, although not all were used on the site. Stone for the prison came from Dartmoor and Portland, and the final average cost of each cell was just over £70. Women were housed at the prison from 1891 until being moved to another prison in 1902, when their places at Wormwood Scrubs were taken by debtors.

Officers from Wormwood Scrubs prison, winners of the Coronation Challenge Cup in 1911, who appear to have competed in a tug-of-war.

The treadmill at Wormwood Scrubs prison in 1895. This non-productive machine was used as an instrument of prison discipline.

Letchford Gardens, probably in the Edwardian era. The ivy-covered building on the right is College Park Library. A reading room was opened there on 22 April 1899 and the library on 9 July 1900. The modern eye is struck by the absence of any parked vehicles or traffic.

Haymaking within sight of Wormwood Scrubs prison, 22 July 1908. The tree is almost obscuring two large haystacks.

The Japan–British Exhibition at the White City, 1910. The Japanese Village can be seen just above the rim of the stadium, which was built for the 1908 Olympic Games.

Demolition of part of the original White City exhibition buildings around 1933 to make way for a new road. The road was initially called Stadium Road, but the name of White City Road came finally to be approved in 1935.

Section Seven

TRANSPORT

John Blight, a taxi driver, of 33 Southerton Road, Hammersmith, c. 1910.

Delivery van no. 4 for Palmer's Stores Ltd of King Street, *c.* 1902. The horse looks well cared for – perhaps more so than those in charge of it!

John Ruff and his hansom cab outside Hammersmith Metropolitan station (now Hammersmith and City Line), 1905. The station frontage has since been rebuilt.

Horse bus in Hammersmith Broadway by The Swan, 1894. Some of the ladies on the bus look less than pleased at having their photograph taken.

Steam wagon *Daisy*, with William Gardner on the left. C.W. Carpenter appears first in local street directories as a 'coal and corn merchant', then as a 'builders' merchant' and finally as a 'haulage contractor' from 1914. The vehicle dates from the Edwardian era, as licence numbers prefixed 'M' were issued from December 1903, but the photograph has a somewhat later date.

A no. 33 motorized bus. Although the location has not been identified and we do not have a definite date for the picture, the advertisement on the side of the bus for *Come Over Here*, which opened at the London Opera House in April 1913, and ran for 217 performances, points to a date just prior to the outbreak of the First World War.

A trolleybus in Beadon Road about to turn into Hammersmith Broadway by The Swan, July 1936.

A Falcon single-deck one-horse tramcar, of the West Metropolitan Tramway Company, outside The Bush Hotel at the junction of Goldhawk Road and Shepherds Bush Green, c. 1891–4. The tram seated sixteen people. Next to the leather-aproned driver is an inspector wearing an official bowler hat and badge.

Uxbridge Road station, West London Railway, at the eastern end of Shepherds Bush Green, c. 1870. Originally known as Shepherds Bush station, it was renamed on 1 November 1869. The station closed in 1940 and was later demolished. The railway line is still in use.

Hammersmith Metropolitan Line station, Beadon Road, with a London United Tramways tram outside, *c.* 1909. Bracket-arm overhead wire suspension, shown here, was little used on the London United Tramways.

Bank holiday travellers waiting for a tram in Goldhawk Road, *c*. 1903. The steps of this tram could not have been easy to climb in the long dresses worn by women then.

Crowds of more would-be travellers outside Uxbridge Road station on August Bank Holiday 1903. This spot has been completely changed by the large roundabout to the east of Shepherds Bush Green.

A caravan of new electric tramcars prepares to leave Shepherds Bush for Southall on the official inauguration of London's first public electric tramway in 1901. Trams 101–9 formed the ceremonial procession, clearly quite a spectacle, which can be seen entering Uxbridge Road.

East Acton station on the Ealing and Shepherds Bush Railway, 1920. Following the construction of a link at Wood Lane and the electrification of the line, passenger services run by the Central London Railway commenced in August 1920. The bricks and other materials behind the station in this photograph were there in preparation for the building of the Wormholt Estate.

A fire in the railway yard between Richford Street and the back of Sulgrave Road in the early 1900s. The photograph was taken by Mr H. Warner from the upstairs window of his home in Richford Street.

The booking office at Shepherds Bush station (Central London Railway), probably during the Edwardian era. This line was known as the Twopenny Tube, a reference to the uniform fare between Shepherds Bush and the Bank. The station opened on 30 July 1900.

The platform at Shepherds Bush station (Central London Railway), *c.* 1903. There appears to be a newspaper stand about half-way along the platform.

Preparing for the Motor Show at Olympia, *c.* 1924. The photograph shows a poignant juxtaposition of the old and the new – a modern car is transported to the show by horses. The first such event held at Olympia was the International Motor Show and Cycle Tournament of 1896.

British Legion outing, *c.* 1920. The charabanc, a rather elongated vehicle, is at Shepherds Bush Green and there is 'another one behind'. The obligatory musician, with concertina, is sitting in the back row.

Section Eight

WAR

Second World War bomb damage at the Peabody Estate in Fulham Palace Road. This incident was caused by a flying bomb, which fell at 3.45 a.m. on 22 August 1944. Fifteen people were killed and thirty-three injured. The notice on the wall of the air-raid shelter offers a £5 reward for the conviction of anyone wilfully damaging the shelter.

A street collection during the Boer War, 1900. The ornamental lanterns and decorations convey a festive atmosphere which jars with the grim reality of fund-raising for the war in South Africa. Even a dog and child's donkey have been pressed into service.

The Lucy Foreman Motor Ambulance, named after the wife of Henry Foreman, Mayor of Hammersmith 1913–20. The Mayor was active in promoting charities during the First World War, and initiated a scheme to provide hospitality for Belgian refugees. Later MP for South Hammersmith, he was knighted in 1921 and died in 1924.

Voluntary Aid Detachment (VAD) ambulances in Ravenscourt Park during the First World War. The VAD was formed in 1909; from 1914 its work was organized by the Red Cross.

Officers of the C Company (Bushmen) of the West London Volunteers, 6 November 1915. Their Hon. Commandant Sir William Bull, MP, is in the centre of the group. The Bushmen were a Home Defence Volunteer Corps of men who were for some reason 'debarred from joining H.M. Regular Forces', and had to provide their own equipment and uniforms, assisted through local fund raising.

Henry Foreman, Hammersmith's mayor, visiting a war canteen. It looks as though a cheque is being handed over, possibly to enable the Red Cross to continue providing comforts for servicemen. Another of Foreman's wartime schemes was to give support to the YMCA for providing a recreation room for troops quartered at White City.

Experiments by the 20th Squadron of the Royal Naval Air Service with a Killen Strait Tractor on Wormwood Scrubs, June 1915. Lloyd George and Winston Churchill watched some of the experiments in which the tractors had been fitted with torpedo wire cutters. The servicemen in this photograph seem to be in a somewhat precarious position!

Building aeroplanes at Waring & Gillow's factory in Cambridge Grove during the First World War. Many factories and other premises were pressed into quite different uses from their peacetime ones as part of the war effort.

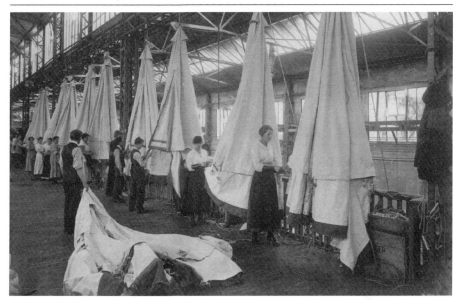

Tent making at another of Waring & Gillow's premises in one of the old exhibition buildings of the White City, during the First World War. Nearly 8,000 people were employed here, mainly in making tents and gas-masks. Anti-gas headpieces were also made for the army's horses.

Another view of Waring & Gillow's aeroplane factory in Cambridge Grove. All those seen working on covering aircraft wings in this picture are women. During the First World War many women found themselves working outside the home for the first time.

Children from Old Oak School, who had been evacuated to Oxford, waiting for the bus to take them to temporary homes at the outbreak of the Second World War in September 1939. The children are all carrying gas-masks and wearing what look like luggage labels to identify themselves.

Bomb damage to The Telegraph pub and houses in Richmond Gardens. Twenty people died in this incident on 26 October 1940, during the Blitz on London. Note the white rings painted round the trees to help people avoid bumping into them in the blackout.

The junction of Uxbridge Road and Askew Crescent, with salvaged furniture on the right. The air raids incidents register, unusually, names the victims of this raid on 25 September 1940: '235 Uxbridge Road is where Dr Fonseca, wife, child and maid killed'.

Nos 121–35 Askew Road after an incident in which twenty-one people died, 25 September 1940. The water and gas mains were broken, as was the trolleybus cable. The blast also blew off some of the shop fronts, revealing the names of previous businesses.

The aftermath of an incident on 18 September 1940, in Starfield Road, in which nine people died. The homeless were evacuated to nearby Westville Road School.

Local residents bringing out their old iron when Hammersmith organized a salvage drive for scrap metal and waste paper in April 1940.

Open-air thanksgiving service for the end of the war in Europe in May 1945, at Ravenscourt Park. The procession was headed by mounted police and the Hammersmith Borough Band (formerly the 43rd Home Guard Battalion), and included the mayor and other dignitaries. The service began with 'O God, our help in ages past' and concluded with 'Now thank we all our God'.

VE Day celebrations in Shepherds Bush, thought to be in Galloway Road. Surprisingly there is only one child to be seen in this photograph, being held up in the centre of the back row. Loudspeakers, radiograms, pianos and wirelesses were set up to provide news and music for the celebrations, which continued into the following day.

Local children enjoying the victory celebrations, 1945. Much ingenuity went into the provision of party foods and suitable decorations. The official announcement of the cease fire had been broadcast by Winston Churchill at 3 p.m. on 8 May 1945.

'Clippies' and a bus conductor celebrate VE Day in Hammersmith Broadway, 1945. Their expressions reveal the overwhelming joy and relief felt throughout the country after six years of war. They were probably based at the bus garage just around the corner in Queen Caroline Street. By midnight on 8 May there were people dancing in the Broadway, and there was also impromptu dancing in Ravenscourt Park.

Section Nine

EDUCATION

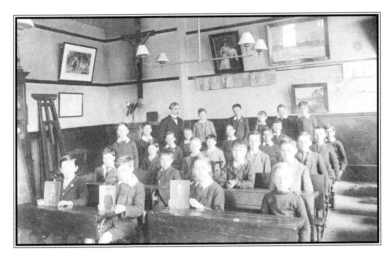

Children at Kenmont Gardens School in College Park, probably during the First World War. The boys in the front row are holding up photographs of men in military uniform, possibly their fathers.

A class of boys from St John's Infants' School with their teacher, c. 1885. Prior to the Second World War the school was situated in Glenthorne Road, close to St John's Church. After it was bombed, on 23 June 1944, the pupils were moved into half of Waterside School in Macbeth Street.

The playground of Elgin House School in Goldhawk Road, c. 1902. A board on the front of the school advertised 'Day and Boarding School for Boys. Pupils thoroughly prepared for business, Civil Service, Oxford & Cambridge Locals, Chamber of Commerce, the Army and Navy & College of Preceptors Examinations . . .'. The school also had a preparatory section for younger boys.

Ellerslie Road Infants' School in 1916. The school was officially opened on 27 August 1894. In this photograph of a class of more than fifty children the girls outnumber the boys, and the two sexes are sitting in separate parts of the room. The teacher in the picture is believed to have been Miss Saltmarsh.

The gymnasium at Brook Green Ladies' College, *c.* 1905. The school was run by the Misses James at 29 Brook Green. Behind the vaulting horse a kettle is sitting on a stove in the fireplace. The trophies on the wall look distinctly unladylike.

The playing fields of St Paul's Girls' School, which opened in Brook Green in 1904. The hockey ball, in this posed photograph of around 1910, is nowhere near the players, who are about to bully off.

The art room at St Paul's Boys' School in Hammersmith Road, 1898. As at least three of the boys are using dividers, it is possible that they are having a geometry or technical drawing lesson rather than an art class. On the rear wall is an illustration of Hammersmith Bridge.

A boxing match in the gymnasium at St Paul's Boys' School, 1932. Photographs of some of the school's sporting teams can be seen. The school moved across the river to Barnes in 1968 and the old red brick building which it had occupied in Hammersmith was demolished two years later. A housing development was built on the site. Only the High Master's house survived.

Class D of Wood Lane Open Air School, April 1931. The school had opened in 1929 with the 'new fangled' idea of open-air classes for delicate children. It was described as a 'model school for youngsters who were victims of asthma and other chest complaints'. The school day was from 9 a.m. to 6 p.m., and pupils were given dinner and tea. As a result of the care they received here, many children were able to return to ordinary schools.

Section Ten

WORK

A consignment of bread about to leave Chibnall's Bakery, Chiswick Mall, on Christmas Eve in the Edwardian period. Public health officers today might well be rather unhappy about the way the bread was exposed to all the elements.

'Popcorn balls' being weighed at Fuller's factory in Great Church Lane, 1910. Fuller's were well-known manufacturers of cakes, chocolates and other delicacies. The business was based in Hammersmith between 1900 and 1965.

Stick finishing and fitting at the Imperial Tobacco Co. Ltd in 1907. The company, known as 'The Civic Co. Ltd' from the mid-1920s, had its premises at the northern end of Fulham Palace Road. It was best known locally for its production of pipes and smokers' requisites.

Bakehouse workers at Chibnall's Bakery, *c.* 1900. The bakery was started in 1897 by J.R. Chibnall. An advertisement of 1914 stated that it was 'noted for high-class confectionery, wedding cakes, home-made and Vienna bread'.

The blacksmith's workshop under the railway arches in Wells Road, off Goldhawk Road, in the early 1900s. The business continued here until the mid-1960s. A few years before its closure the blacksmith, Tom Williams – still working under the business name of R. Lovell – continued to shoe horses belonging to rag-and-bone men and one or two greengrocers, as well as doing a lot of 'wedding work'.

The pressroom of the shared premises of the Doves Bindery and the Doves Press at 15 Upper Mall, *c.* 1911. On the left is Albert Lewis and on the right is Henry Gage-Cole. The Doves Press was founded in 1900 by T.J. Cobden-Sanderson and Emery Walker; their working relationship was not easy and Emery Walker retired from the partnership in 1909. In 1917 Cobden-Sanderson threw the matrices, punches and types of the Doves Press into the Thames so that no one else could use them.

The family of Walter Ward, builder and decorator, of 364 King Street, in 1908. Walter, aged sixty-three, is shown with his nine sons, all of whom had been working on one job when this photograph was taken. From left to right: Sydney, Arthur, Edward, George, Walter (senior), Walter (junior), Ernest, Frederick, Charlie and Cecil. Walter (senior) – who had known William Morris – had sixteen children in all, three daughters in addition to the nine sons depicted plus four children who died in infancy.

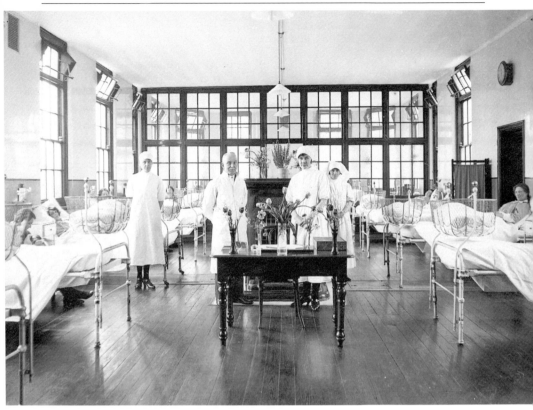

The maternity ward at Hammersmith Hospital in 1927. Note the cribs suspended at the end of each bed. The hospital was originally part of Hammersmith Workhouse, which had opened in 1905. At the time there was criticism of the amount of money spent on providing a high standard of accommodation for the poor, with the workhouse becoming known locally as the 'Pauper's Palace'.

Police officers at the rear of Askew Road police station in 1922. The station was in 'F' Division and closed after the Home Office decided, in 1971, that it was surplus to requirements. Askew Library opened on the site in 1975.

Brushmaking at 160 Railway Approach, under the railway arches between Uxbridge Road and Goldhawk Road, in the 1920s. Albert Young had his workshop here around 1919–26. Until the introduction of nylon and other synthetic materials, brushmakers were entirely dependent on animals as the source of the bristles they required, the finest brushes being made from badger hair. Simple machinery for the manufacture of some types of brushes was introduced around 1875, but in this photograph all the work is being done by hand.

William A. Cole with two apprentices in his boatyard in Upper Mall, probably during the 1930s. The business came under threat in 1935, when plans to develop what was a very run-down area were put forward by Hammersmith Borough Council. The boatyard had, according to the newspapers of the day, a traceable history of 134 years.

Part of the fleet of Ford vehicles owned by George Wimpey & Co. in 1932. E. Beresford, then assistant company director, can be seen with the company's new 14.9 h.p. Ford Tudor saloon cars in Hammersmith Grove.

Tracks being laid in Goldhawk Road in 1898, ready for London's first electric tramway which came into operation in 1901. The London United Tramway Company had taken over existing horse-tram lines, and these were relaid with heavier rails ready for the introduction of electric trams. The work was contracted to George Wimpey & Co., and Mr Wimpey can be seen in the centre of the photograph wearing a light-coloured hat. Wimpey's began in Hammersmith in 1880 when George Wimpey established a stone working business with William Tomes. Their yard in Hammersmith Grove was situated close to Grove Road station, an ideal location as materials could easily be received there from quarries all over the country.

The yard of Glover's Dairy Farm at 15 Brook Green Road (now Shepherds Bush Road) in 1910. Walter Glover, the dairy manager, is in the centre of the picture, wearing a straw boater. Various sized cans for measuring out the milk are hanging from the sides of the milk floats. The dairy was purchased by the Express Dairy Company in 1928.

The soup kitchen queue at South Street Mission in the 1930s, which was a period of hardship for many people unable to find work. South Street Mission was founded in 1900 by Dalling Road Primitive Methodist Church and West End Baptist Church. The present building, in Macbeth Street, opened on 4 December 1930.

A new boat for the Oxford crew being built for the Oxford and Cambridge Universities Boat Race which took place on 29 March 1947. It is being built at the boathouse of Mr G. Sims (on the left in this photograph) in Lower Mall. A boat was also built here for the Cambridge crew.

Dowel & Son of 3 Ravenscourt Avenue, probably early this century. Watering cans, trowels, forks and other gardening implements are displayed in the right-hand window, and in the left-hand window 'best lawn grass seeds' are being offered for sale. The business was here for about forty years from the mid-1890s onwards.

No. 110–110a Uxbridge Road, a confectioner's shop and tobacconist's shop seen side-by-side, c. 1906. Nowadays these functions are usually combined. The notice in the window indicates that Mr Arthur Studley had previously been at 62 Uxbridge Road.

Grover's Stores at 89 Hammersmith Grove during the First World War. The female members of the family ran the business during this period.

Capps, the greengrocers, of 123 Hammersmith Road, *c.* 1900. The shopkeeper in this photograph, wearing an apron, was Henry Dazeley. The shop was opposite Cadby Hall, whose sign 'Cadby Hall, J. Lyons' can be seen reflected in the shop window. The business was here from the 1890s to the 1920s.

One of the many horses owned by the Borough Engineer's Department of Hammersmith Council, probably photographed during the 1930s. In 1900 the council owned sixty-five horses which had been bought for sums between £40 and £72 each; the cost of feeding them in the previous year was £1,878. The oldest horse in 1900, aged twenty-one, had been employed for almost fourteen years.

The staff of Hammersmith Reference Library photographed by the borough librarian, Mr H.P. Dinelli, *c.* 1912–13. E.E. Larner (centre), who had been employed by the council from the age of thirteen, was well known as a walker. He came fifth in the 10-mile walk in the 1908 Olympic Games held at White City.

A meeting of Hammersmith Borough Council in session at the old Hammersmith Town Hall in Brook Green Road (now Shepherds Bush Road). Sir Marshall Hayes, who was mayor 1920–5, is seated in the centre under the clock. Sir William Bull, MP, is the third person to his left. The clock was a gift to the council in 1917, and had originally stood at the entrance to the Great Exhibition of 1851 in Hyde Park.

Washing stalls at the Lime Grove Baths and Wash-houses, *c.* 1948–9. The baths opened in 1908. In 1949 they were described as a place where 'the public can at very small cost avail themselves of up-to-date facilities for washing, drying and mangling, and a feature of the ironing rooms are the modern electric irons'. Launderettes and home washing machines subsequently sounded the death knell of this type of municipal enterprise.

A Ministry of Food Welfare Foods van parked in Downs Place, off King Street, in June 1947. Work for many women meant housework and bringing up children. Here mothers are seen collecting orange juice, cod liver oil and vitamin tablets to improve the health of their families.

ENTERTAINMENT
AND LEISURE

The open-air dance floor which had just opened at Playlands at the White City in July 1934. The floor was situated under the giant scenic railway and the photograph shows a cabaret turn in progress.

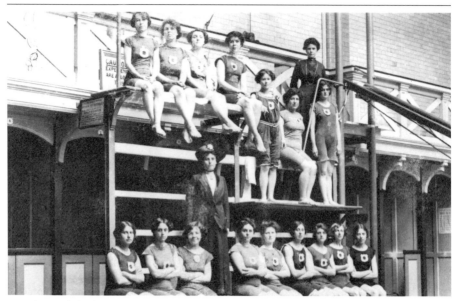

Members of the ladies' swimming section of the Star Athletics Club in 1913. The club was founded in 1898 and the ladies' swimming section was created in 1902. In their first appearance in a race at the club's gala they caused a 'considerable sensation'.

Members of the gentlemen's swimming section of the Star Athletics Club with Sir William Bull, MP, by the long-distance shield, *c.* 1920. Long-distance races were regularly held in the Thames. The ladies' section competed in 1910 in the first known ladies' 'clothes race', in which competitors swam a quarter of a mile fully clothed.

The 1935–6 Queens Park Rangers football team. The club was officially formed, in 1886, after the merger of the two teams of St Jude's Institute and Christ Church Rangers. At the time this photograph was taken QPR were playing in Division 3 South. Back row (left to right): Harry Lowe, H. Schofield, Albert Blake, William (Bill) Carr, Pat Molloy and Alec Farmer. Third row: D. Richards (trainer), James Allen, Sidney Russell, Walter Barrie, William (Bill) S. Mason, Sam Abel, Frederick Bartlett, Ernie Vincent and Jimmy Eggleton (assistant trainer). Second row: Tommy Cheetham, Frank Lumsden, Jack Fletcher, Jonty Rowe, Billy Birrell (secretary-manager), Johnny Ballantyne, David Samuel, David Ovenstone and Joseph Hammond. Front row: John Forsyth Crawford, Richard (Dicky) March and Charlie Clark.

Members of the Hammersmith St Paul's Football Club, 1907–8 season. A number of professional football clubs, like Fulham Football Club and Queens Park Rangers, owe their origins to church clubs and other youth organizations. Back row (left to right): F.A. Roberts, L. Lloyd, F.T. Gilkes, G. Hart, R. Howell, H.E. Harding, N. Hammond, E. Atkinson, W.H. Cooper and E. Rawkins. Centre row: D.J. D'eath, A.E. Holliss (hon. sec.), Revd E.S. Duval (captain), Revd G.N. Walsh (president), P.W. Darby (vice-captain), P. Snook and H.G. Bickers. Front row: H. Moffatt, V. Marshall, S. Daniells, W. Baker and E.J. Mussett.

An apparently gentle game of croquet on the lawn of Rivercourt House, 36 Upper Mall, in 1869. The lawn was kept in its pristine state by a two-handed mowing machine. In this picture one gardener is pushing the mower while the second is using a rope to pull it along.

The skittle alley at The Black Lion on 8 June 1928, showing a match in progress. The author Sir Alan Herbert ('A.P.H.') was president of the skittle club for thirty years, and described a skittle alley, possibly this one, in his book *The Water Gipsies*. He is in the back row of the spectators, standing seventh from the left.

The Brotherhood Orchestra of Shepherds Bush Baptist Tabernacle, *c.* 1910–14. The Brotherhood was in existence from about 1910 onwards. The proceeds of their Christmas Cheer concerts were used for the help and comfort of the sick and needy at Christmas time.

The original caption on the back of this photograph is '40 (winks) not out'. It depicts members of the Hammersmith Cricket Club, which seems to have consisted largely of councillors and council officers, at a match on 19 July 1906. The ground now forms part of Latymer Upper School's playing fields. From left to right: Councillor Green, the mayor; Alderman T. Chamberlen; and the town clerk, Mr Thompson.

Members of the Hammersmith Cricket Club outside their pavilion, probably in the mid-1890s. The pavilion was located near the junction of Wood Lane and Du Cane Road. The date on the pavilion is thought to relate to its opening, rather than the year in which the members were photographed, as it features in several post-1890s photographs. The *West London Observer*, in 1889, mentions that the club is playing in its eighth season. It seems likely that it had existed on an unofficial basis for some years before this, as Hammersmith Vestrymen and members of the Board of Works had regularly played an annual cricket match against Watson, Sons & Room, a firm of local solicitors.

The dance floor at the Hammersmith Palais in Brook Green Road, shortly after its opening at the end of 1919. The Palais became an ice-rink from 1929 to 1933, and continues today as a popular dance venue. The first bands to play there were the Original Dixieland Jazz Band and Billy Arnold's American Novelty Band.

Ice skating at the old Hammersmith Palais de Danse in 1930. The ice rink opened on 30 December 1929 after extensive work had been carried out on the dance hall. There were three skating sessions each day at the Ice Drome, and a new ice cabaret was produced each week. Lessons were available at a charge of 2s 6d.

King's Theatre, Hammersmith Road, October 1903. The theatre had a seating capacity of 3,000 and opened on 26 December 1902 with a production of *Cinderella*. The theatre was a popular venue, but closed in 1955. After a short period as a television studio it was demolished in 1963. Modern office buildings now occupy the site, at the junction with Rowan Road.

Stage hands of the Lyric Opera House, later the Lyric Theatre, rebuilt in 1895 to seat 775 people. The photograph was taken on 26 December 1897. The present-day Lyric Theatre, close to the site of the original, is located within a shopping development and incorporates much of the original elaborate Victorian plasterwork. The seating capacity at its re-opening in 1979 was 537.

The Shepherds Bush Empire pictured on a spring day early this century. Opened in 1903, it was mainly used for music-hall turns. After its closure in 1953 it was used by the BBC for recording many television favourites, including the *Billy Cotton Band Show* and *Crackerjack*. The BBC gave up the building in 1991; since then it has been refurbished and is now used as a venue for rock and pop concerts.

The Scala Cinema at 255 Hammersmith Road in September 1921. The advertising efforts of the sandwich-board men, pictured here, were obviously successful, as the commissionaire is standing by a 'full-house' notice. The cinema had various names between 1908 and its closure in the early 1930s, including Theatre de Luxe, Bio-Cinema, Star and Cosy. Butterwick, part of the Hammersmith Broadway one-way road system, now covers this site.

Staff of the Gaumont Palace Cinema in Hammersmith Broadway, photographed in the mid-1930s. The cinema opened on 28 March 1932 with the enormous seating capacity of 4,000. Going to the cinema was an immensely popular pastime at this period. Later known as the Hammersmith Odeon and now named The Apollo, it is used as a venue for rock and pop concerts. Included here are the manager, Mr Reed (fifth from the right in the front row) and the projectionist, Arthur James Clements (third from the left, fourth row back).

The Flip Flap at the Franco-British Exhibition at the White City, 1908. This was a novelty ride costing 6*d*. After a signal the carriages, which seated forty-eight people, started to move up. At a height of 200 feet they passed each other and descended to the other side. The trip took all of three minutes. The machine was designed by Mr Imre Kiralfy, who created the exhibition. The views from the top of its arc must have been quite breathtaking.

A maiden of coy disposition
Met her fate at the Bush Exhibition.
When his great love he told her.
Placed her head on his shoulder
And enjoyed the happy position.

Novelty postcards featuring the Franco-British Exhibition and pretty girls were very popular. This card was captioned 'You mustn't believe everything you hear about the Franco'. The exhibition contained a clever mixture of educational and fun features, and was well attended. On the opening day, 14 May 1908, 123,000 people crowded onto the site. Admission was one shilling for a day, and season tickets costing £1 1s 0d for adults were available. The all-white exhibition buildings soon earned the nickname of The White City.

Taking the dog for a run. Greyhound racing started at White City stadium – which had been built for the 1908 Olympic Games – on 20 June 1927, with an attendance of 20,000 people. In this 1930s picture novice greyhounds are having their first trial run at White City.

Maintenance work on the electric hare at White City Stadium in the mid-1930s. The hare could travel at 40 m.p.h. In 1945 a camera was installed to record close finishes, and could provide judges with a photograph in 38 seconds.

The draw by Miss Jocelyn Sparks, a 'Society hostess', for the first heats of the Greyhound Grand National, which was to be run a few days later at White City. The draw, at the Prince of Wales Theatre, was made on the 24 May 1934.

Anna Lee, the film star, presenting the Annual Long Distance Trophy to Mrs J. Hopkins. Her greyhound, Congleton Lord, had broken the national record for 725 yards at the White City Stadium in August 1938. He looks very pleased with himself!

The Belgrave Harriers competing in an eight-hour walking race at the White City on 29 September 1933. Fifteen leading British walkers competed in 'a mass attack on track records'. Tommy Green, the 1932 Olympic Gold Medallist at 50 km, and winner of the London to Brighton Race in 1929–31 and 1933, had to retire from the race through illness. Two new walking records were set that day.

Mae West the mule, renowned for her ability to imitate the movements of her owner Homer Holcombe. The photograph shows her impersonating Tishy, a famous 'cross-legged' horse, at the White City Stadium during the World Championship Rodeo, 29 June 1934.

Peggy Worth, the actress, and her Italian fiancé the Marquis Vincenzo Regoli di Monali, in the front seat of car no. 4 on the water chute at Playlands, 28 June 1934. Playlands was London's newest pleasure ground (see p. 2).

Young ladies enjoying themselves at the miniature Brooklands speedway at Playlands, in 1934.

Lilian La Bram with her partner, The Great Samson. Apart from performing astounding acrobatic feats in mid-air, their main act was for Lilian to be shot from a cannon and caught by hand without the use of nets. This 'sensational' act was another of the attractions at Playlands. Some of the old White City exhibition buildings can be seen on the left of the photograph, which was taken on 29 April 1934.

A game of pitch-and-toss being played by youngsters on Shepherds Bush Green in 1910. Petty gambling was one of the social problems associated with the Green at this period, and was doubtless linked to the number of people sleeping rough there (see p. 66).

Section Twelve

SPECIAL

OCCASIONS

*Field Marshal Montgomery visiting Hammersmith, 5 March 1949. He is standing
alongside Hammersmith's mayor, Alderman R.J. Buckingham, outside the Gaumont
Cinema, before giving a talk to local children. Later he was to visit the Regal Cinema to
receive the Freedom of Hammersmith and then to inaugurate 'Hammersmith Week'.*

'Jubilation in the traditional manner'. The bonfire built to celebrate the coronation of King Edward VII on 26 June 1902. The coronation was postponed to 9 August 1902 because of the King's illness. A note on the back of the original copy of this photograph reads 'by some mischance the bonfire was set alight before the date was finally settled'. Reports of the coronation celebrations, when they eventually took place, make no mention of the bonfire, so presumably it was not replaced.

The London to Manchester Aeroplane Race which took place in April 1910. The race was between Claude Grahame-White and the Frenchman Louis Paulham. Paulham won the substantial prize of £10,000 for the race, which was organized by the *Daily Mail*. The top photograph shows Grahame-White's Henry Farman biplane, and the bottom photograph shows him seated in it.

The unveiling of the Hammersmith War Memorial, a bronze winged figure of Peace, at the eastern end of Shepherds Bush Green on 11 November 1922 – exactly four years after the end of the First World War – by General Sir Charles Munro. A letter in the *West London Observer* commented unfavourably on the traffic noises intruding into the ceremony.

The official opening of Shepherds Bush Library on 25 June 1896. The building, designed by Maurice B. Adams, was a gift to the borough from Mr John Passmore Edwards, the wealthy philanthropist who financed the building of seventy libraries, convalescent homes, hospitals and other public buildings. He had laid the foundation stone of this library on 4 July 1895. The opening ceremony was performed by Lord Rosebery. As was not unusual in those days, living accommodation – with its own separate entrance – was provided for the librarian in charge.

The Scots Greys passing through Shepherds Bush, photographed near the junction of Uxbridge Road and Wood Lane, on their way to the coronation of King George V and Queen Mary on 22 June 1911.

The official opening of Uxbridge Road Baptist Tabernacle by the mayor, Mr J.J.R. Green, on 1 May 1906. Designed by R. Norman Hewitt, the church was built by the local firm of T.E. Mills & Son for just over £3,000. It was destroyed by bombs on 13 October 1940 and replaced by a new church in September 1956.

Another official opening, this time of the open space in St Peter's Square. Surrounded by attractive houses built around 1825–30, the original open space was designed by the landscape gardener J.C. Loudon and had contained an artesian well. For some years prior to 1913 the gardens were overgrown and contained a board offering the land for sale. Only when the board was removed and building operations commenced was there a public outcry. The council acquired the land for use as a public open space in December 1913 and the formal opening was performed by the mayor, Henry Foreman, on 29 April 1915. Seated to the left of the mayor are Councillor Charles Pascall, Admiral Sir Edmund Robert Fremantle and Leslie Gordon, the town clerk.

St Paul's School on the occasion of the unveiling, by Lord Roberts, of the South African War Memorial on 29 May 1906. Two hundred and twenty Old Paulines, of whom eleven died, fought in the Boer War. The memorial bore the names of those who were killed, on the copper panels surrounding the fountain in the centre.

The mayor and mayoress, Councillor Arthur and Mrs Belsham, attending the Silver Jubilee celebrations of King George V and Queen Mary in Beavor Lane, June 1935. Judging from local newspaper reports the mayor and mayoress seem to have spent most of the first half of June attending celebratory tea parties.

The Silver Jubilee drive of King George V and Queen Mary passing through Hammersmith Broadway on 8 June 1935. The affection with which they were regarded shows itself in the large number of people lining the route and the proliferation of decorations. The first part of the drive was in a motor car, then at Hortensia Road, Chelsea, the King and Queen boarded an open landau. Their route through Hammersmith was from Fulham Palace Road into Hammersmith Broadway, Brook Green Road, Brook Green, Hammersmith Road and from there into Kensington.

Members of the Hammersmith Socialist Society in the garden of Kelmscott House. The photograph was probably taken shortly after the Hammersmith branch of the Socialist League withdrew to form the Hammersmith Socialist Society in November 1891. William Morris, with his distinctive beard, and his daughter May are in the front row. He is seated next to the lady with the striped skirt. Others in the photograph are Emery Walker, T.J. Cobden-Sanderson and Halliday Sparling.

Money arriving, with an armed guard, for the Christmas 1939 share-out of the Broadway Congregational Friendly Society at the Westminster Bank (now National Westminster Bank), King Street. The society, which was founded in 1905, shared out £67,000 between 20,000 investors.

The symbolic laying of the foundation stone of the new Royal Masonic Hospital at Olympia on 19 May 1932. This ceremony was organized to enable Freemasons from all over the country to commemorate the event, as there was insufficient space for them all at the actual site. The real foundation stone was laid, at the same time, at the hospital site by the Duke of Connaught and Strathearn. The hospital, near Ravenscourt Park, has been a well-known local institution for over sixty years, but its future is now uncertain.

Field Marshal Montgomery leaving the Gaumont Cinema (now The Apollo), Hammersmith Broadway, on 5 March 1949. The next stop on his visit was to inspect a guard of honour at Hammersmith Town Hall before receiving the Freedom of Hammersmith (see also p. 145).

West London Hospital's 'Pound Day', 21 June 1939. Children are putting their gifts for the hospital into special bins at the Hammersmith Palais de Danse. The mayor, Alderman William Church, and the comedian Lupino Lane are looking on.

Mrs Wyatt of Batoum Gardens, clutching her identity card, receiving a gift of tinned foods from the Lord Mayor of Sydney, Alderman R.J. Bartley, and Hammersmith's mayor, Alderman R.J. Buckingham, on 10 October 1947. Food parcels were sent to Hammersmith as a gift for 250 old-age pensioners by the people of New South Wales, Australia. The immediate post-war period, with food and other items continuing to be rationed, was a time of austerity and hardship for many people.

An open-air meeting of the British Union at Shepherds Bush, in Stanlake Road, 25 September 1938. Sir Oswald Mosley, seen giving the Fascist salute, spoke from the top of a large motor van equipped with loudspeakers. At the end of the meeting the main body of the crowd marched away loudly shouting 'we want peace'. Contrary to expectations there were no disturbances, and only two youths were removed from the crowd by police.

Three nuns arriving to vote in the South Hammersmith by-election, 24 February 1949, held following the death of the local MP, W.T. Adams. The election was won by the Labour candidate, William T. Williams.

The American film star, Tallulah Bankhead, surrounded by various guests and dignitaries at the laying of the foundation stone of the Commodore Cinema in King Street, on New Year's Day 1929. The cinema, which was designed by George Coles and seated over 3,000 people, opened on 14 September of that year. The souvenir opening brochure described the Commodore as 'London's supreme talkie theatre'. Five million bricks, fifteen tons of steel and twenty miles of cable went into its construction. The cinema had its own organist, Harry Davidson, and a resident orchestra. It closed in June 1963 and re-opened almost immediately as a bingo hall. Offices now occupy the site. Pictured from left to right in the front row of the photograph are Sir Charles Sykes, Mrs B.J. Samels (mayoress), Mrs Jack de Leon, Jack de Leon, Tallulah Bankhead and Alderman B.J. Samels (mayor). None of the other guests has been identified.

Farewell to the King. Mourners at Wormwood Scrubs await the passing of the train bearing the body of King Edward VII to Windsor, 20 May 1910. The men have taken off their hats as a token of respect.

Acknowledgements

All the pictures in this book have been selected from the collection of more than 60,000 photographs held at Hammersmith and Fulham Archives and Local History Centre. This superb collection owes much to the numerous individuals who have enriched it over the years by donating their own photographs, or loaning them for copying, and whose acts of generosity have thus preserved for posterity these images of the past.

Thanks are offered in particular to the following for granting permission to reproduce certain photographs in this book, with apologies for any omissions:

Mr A.J. Clements • Mrs F.K. Dazeley MBE • Mrs M. Holser
Imperial War Museum • Mr B. Nicholls • Shaftesbury Society
Mrs P.D. Spencer • Mrs K. Westley • George Wimpey plc.

Our greatest debt of gratitude, however, is to those photographers of the past whose pictorial records of Hammersmith and Shepherds Bush are reproduced here. Their names are, in most cases, unrecorded; but without them this book would not have been possible.